Day of the Child

Also by ARRA LYNN ROSS

Seedlip and Sweet Apple

Day of the Child

a
poem ARRA LYNN ROSS

MILKWEED EDITIONS

Published 2021 by Milkweed Editions
Printed in the United States of America
Cover design by Mary Austin Speaker
Cover art by Max Ross Kidder
21 22 23 24 25   5 4 3 2 1
First Edition

Milkweed Editions, an independent nonprofit publisher, gratefully acknowledges sustaining support from our Board of Directors; the Alan B. Slifka Foundation and its president, Riva Ariella Ritvo-Slifka; the Amazon Literary Partnership; the Ballard Spahr Foundation; *Copper Nickel*; the McKnight Foundation; the National Endowment for the Arts; the National Poetry Series; the Target Foundation; and other generous contributions from foundations, corporations, and individuals. Also, this activity is made possible by the voters of Minnesota through a Minnesota State Arts Board Operating Support grant, thanks to a legislative appropriation from the arts and cultural heritage fund. For a full listing of Milkweed Editions supporters, please visit milkweed.org.

Library of Congress Cataloging-in-Publication Data

Names: Ross, Arra Lynn, 1977- author.
Title: Day of the child : a poem / Arra Lynn Ross.
Description: First Edition. | Minneapolis, Minnesota : Milkweed Editions, 2021. |
    Summary: "From Arra Lynn Ross, a tender, generous, and generative extended
    poem centered on the experience of parenthood"-- Provided by publisher.
Identifiers: LCCN 2021011928 (print) | LCCN 2021011929 (ebook) | ISBN
    9781571315373 (paperback) | ISBN 9781571317506 (ebook)
Subjects: LCGFT: Poetry.
Classification: LCC PS3618.O84524 D39 2021 (print) | LCC PS3618.O84524
    (ebook) | DDC 811/.6--dc23
LC record available at https://lccn.loc.gov/2021011928
LC ebook record available at https://lccn.loc.gov/2021011929

Milkweed Editions is committed to ecological stewardship. We strive to align our book production practices with this principle, and to reduce the impact of our operations in the environment. We are a member of the Green Press Initiative, a nonprofit coalition of publishers, manufacturers, and authors working to protect the world's endangered forests and conserve natural resources. *Day of the Child* was printed on acid-free 100% postconsumer-waste paper by McNaughton & Gunn.

for Max

CONTENTS

a poem

...living art,

Which thus presents, and thus records true life.

— Elizabeth Barrett Browning

Day of the Child

1 |

The time-passing: your waterproof watch reads
eight thirty-seven, *exact,* and us late,
your backpack and lunch dangling
as you light the numbers to wait:
pink and green, glowing, now in seconds the change
to eight as your fingers, on buttons, range;
us still, the hall, late,
You: "Exactly eight minutes late!" Given: Time's taut seeds.

2 |

Outside this Small Town springs into sparse bloom:
cold, morning low, slows the tracks of redbud
and curls to ground tulips
whose petals shove above mud.
Driving home, I hear the jury is set
to decide – for Dzhokhar Tsarnaev—death
or prison in life. A boy's blood,
took that bomb. *So young,* said the nun. Morals, said Hume,

3 |

derive not first from reason. Of Passion,
and passion's pleasure, our actions; tempered
by something: sympathy's
blood-stained cloth applied to the hurt bird.
What is learned? I'll return for my son;
at school, at three thirty-eight, bells will ring & run
days over years; but each second
make me not a stranger to abundance' ration.

4 |

Start with laughter in the night, deep in dream;
you, shaking with joy as small saliva
slips over your cracked lip
and shines. Your sweat so Alive ah
clings to too-long curls you will not cut though they brush
eyelids. By day, no, but now I can push
their damp from your forehead,
and kiss & kiss your hot cheeks   as much as I please.

5 |

By the time you are five, we make metaphors
for our love. You are *as a star sweet*. As much
as *the grains of   all sand;*
airy dandelions, their seeds. More:
age seven, the box inside you've slept for nights,
the universe, and I laying beside squashed tight
and tired, only mumble
yes, more than, not *aching thorns*, shoulder pressed to the floor

6 |

(turned, by morning: *love is a circl[e] round*
as a Ball. Love is tr[y]ing to get out
and Don't let it Do that
or you will fall. No slow doubt
stutters your grip on the steady pen, & quick,
a poem for the watch, then *watch!* Magic trick:
Three blue cups, yellow ball
gone under which? Wave the wand and lift), my hidden frown.

7 |

You move too fast to catch, erasing, from mind,
your slight of hand; hard to sustain such attention
when, for years, my self
gave way for your form's extension.
You were river, when I, the river-bank –
young wine, you were, when I, the withered flank –
Mycorrhizae, my wild gentian,
symbiosis – *together-life* – the better bind.

8 |

Scrunched to the bed's edge, your slim shoulders again shrug,
the shaking fake, I'm sure, silvered in too-late light,
head bent over the edge
and drawn to knees, the belly tight.
The rising ire that seethes, then sings caught now between teeth
as you creep close and lay your cheek and arm beneath
my propped pillow. Lowers, night
on mother and son, after the sopping hug.

9 |

Go back to the boy jumping in barn hay,
the smell of twine & sun & raw wood, the smell of laughter
as the spotted piglet
gets in the bin feeder – after,
from the metal hatch his snout poking pink
each time the other tried to feed, or drink.
Could be, from a patched rafter,
looped, a foot, a low rope, from bale to bale made way;

10 |

or to the eclipse, back, earth's shadow high
on moon's right side, sinking, on grass's dark glint,
the locusts bare and our breath
steaming as moon unslivers from earth's rinse.
These minutes all leanings & leavings limned
(on my lap, light in arms; I rub your limbs)
through vast air, the veils, stripped
to reveal, immense and loving, an eye.

11 |

Again, morning's make: walking, a mother deer
downstream with her two spotted fawns, far shore
nibbling sumac greens,
when you: *God gave us those* – four,
no church-taught God, so I urge more for my learning:
She wants to tell us she loves us   turning
circles by the glass door
where later: *why war?* shouting   *I dance with fear*

12 |

and socks! Stomping, with stuffed puppy, and sword:
"I'm breaking the earth. I'm destroying the earth.
I smashed his head off.
Cuts— forty pieces. We have work
to do – no talkin' 'bout sad things. Like that move,
puppy?" Launched high and flying, as to prove
his intention's worth:
"Live free and in the wild!" Where first— hitting the floor – he soared —

13 |

Uphold heaven—humble & hurting, here—rapt
attention the leaven, the un-shunned, sure-
thing, that simple ease
that keeps us shepherds of each pure purr:
where damp ferns uncurl violets, dew-feathered,
and you, freckled with hair flying, untethered,
leap into the azure
air bounding above the trampoline's black clap.

14 |

Joy's map: blooms June – that push-off! Poppy's paper pods
uncrumple, doubled, till sun on dark stamens
purple-black fringed velvet – rings
the fat green pistil, soon sends
blue pollen to brush stigma's softest star:
self-appeasing, self-delighting, nothing can mar
its own sweet will – Heaven's
an orange poppy! And us, tripped of facades, gods.

15 |

More magic: Morning. *Choose a card, remember*
(two, hearts). Slip behind my back the pile, to find
your card? —No. – *But ah, look here:*
in the spread, this one turned over;
take it, sir, ma'am, your chosen – heart
from all the rest, remembered from the very start.
– A sly trick, my dear,
quick of hand & eye, boy of mine, born bright of embers.

16 |

(Or) tender taproot   through gravel, rocks, feeling
for fertile seams. Growing's a force like god,
and I, milked through,
fear am most obstacle to you.
And yet, provide, I, what I can: from the top shelf,
lift the glass jar down, full, creamy white, pour – in delft –
fresh from the cow,
sustenance though   unkind perhaps, times, my dealing.

17 |

Early light winds loose the air balloon curtains,
against the torn screen presses and release
like you at breast—
from your mouth's milk corners, seep,
wipe, I, with cloth, one-handed, fold length-wise
across my thigh; then cradle, shift, your size a guise
I can't see beyond:
seemed eternal, the loose fists, May rain, the day's milk stains

18 |

a refrain I reframed each day with new words:
a finger, wet, running the wine glasses' rims
for water's pitch: *listen*
how   of   late   afternoons move through sand
sound strange & lonely I am, repeating *more*
and *want*, as the grains sift and sift – a bore
of golden light through leaves (needs)
as swinging, your legs hang down; over we, sing the birds.

19 |

Inside me I saw your heart. Made visible
by sound and sound's echo, the living muscle
through its contractions moved –
a frieze on screen. All else, bustle
and talk, small. But a heart! Inside. Of mine – not
mine – by my body's lambent knowledge wrought
your blood pump hustled
and sang O indivisible   divisible

20 |

that, weeks later, split my skin, a sheath, off
but first, the Fire   asked to see the crowning,
I said no (blind my eyes)
but mirror-pressed, your blurry crumpled head
dark-hair touched, wet mound, talked-through thrust
till shit slid, and I, blood-rust—tore—till dust
as empty, then — Plenty:
your dark eyes sharks, and skin oh skin! as soft as loss.

Seven years blink: on river, rain's ink and bow
over the willow arches, double:
There's the invisible being.
Remember, mom? The scar-faced girl
kindled the fire. She married – curve dwindles –
the invisible being – spindles
of pigments past seeing:
    — No, tell me — *Beebo BEE We read it in Poopendale!*

Evening. Showering at top-lung: I am
the Yeti: I am *not* the Yeti! On repeat
over the high-pitched plash
of water on skin, on porcelain.
Unknown composite of influences –
at two, at three, I still walked those fences—
of hand or body, tilt
and lilt of laugh could pick out of who my lamb

23 |

made meal. Of butterflies & milkweed & moon.
In the red wagon, in new snow, I pulled
the evening sky
for you   the dusty plums pitted,
wild, in August's dry corn. Bent, where they clung,
the branch, down for fingers signing *more*: our tongue
of dusk's sun patterned
as winds in fields rose and herds stirred us   home soon –

24 |

Months. Years. Minutes. In thin night, a child crosses
razor wire: refugee: he hears the shouts
above gun-fire—a boy's
not far – as his father pulls him through.
Kitchen table radio talks now routes:
the sunken boats to Greece, the fence finished
at Hungary's border. What light diminished
on the sleepy limbs, what dew
on small hairs drew their clear beads as the child tosses?

25 |

My own: on the hard floor, refuses
the pillow proffered, pushes my hug
away. —I return
to reading, aloud, the ruses
devised by Mrs. Piggle-Wiggle
to cure children of poor behavior –
quiet, soon quick, – wriggle
in beside me; he's burnt through   his fuses

26 |

and wants to sleep – soft and sweet again – alone.
My heart does moan at tender eye, shutting
the door, to open in dream:
of wild horses and flying
birds, one whispers   father's old formula
of this minute makes soft vales – Blake's Beulah
of honey and cream
opening ever inward   on meadows of roan

27 |

and dappled bay until the river, morning gray,
brightens to tarnished silver, no sun blush,
while you scribble your spelling:
explicit a word for bonus,
and *infer*, among the *willing*, the *missed*,
among the *still* and the *different*, a list
of doubled letters
that *balloon* above the night horse's neigh.

28 |

October thirtieth, two-thousand fifteen.
A Friday. Your reaper's robe folded, in the bag,
for school's noon parade.
The white mask and squeezable heart
on the bed, left; and too, the scythe – forbidden
so I've sewn black cloth in the hood, hidden
your face, a blank, a part
of the dark masquerade —you see but are not seen.

29 |

The thread thins. December. Paris.
After the bombings, the climate talks.
Who bears the burdens
of finance, the limits of degree?
"Well below 2C" ensures humanity?
School-bound, I explain denial's inanity,
Money trumps Truth's decree?
To tell   the earth's young inheritor   does embarrass—

30 |

Listening, he's creased Friday's popcorn dollar
twice, lengthwise, along Washington's green face:
tilted up, the brows arch:
"I'm so happy! I want to murder!"
my son says, then turns it down: "I'm so sad."
"I have no home." Tilt, again to glad
"Murder!" Down: Trodden. "Brrr."
How quick, his grasp of complicity, of squalor.

31 |

— Fine snow settles on the locusts' fallen branches;
dark-eyed junco, white-breast of roses,
flits beneath mulberry,
black walnut, while ice islands thicken
over the river's perpetual gesture;
their lace, stately, an investiture:
visible cold, quicken
our blood—gone deep to heat the heart   the rest, resting, blanches

32 |

though from warm islands, back, from rain and sand
where, slathered, you ran the rim, footprints filling
with the sizzle of salt tide;
where, from high branches, down you knocked
green coconuts so, lifting your machete –
honed clean on the concrete curb – you steady
and aim, eyes locked
until the blade through flesh and wooded husk does land –

33 |

in plastic cups the milky liquid poured,
your proud offering for all. We drink it down,
bits of sand, husk, all.
Quantum theory says time is always:
each moment has always been, will always be:
bright islands in the sea. Great currents: you, me.
Always, the green ball
in the street's pink petals. You, unmade; yet there, adored.

34 |

The arrow of time pierces this point: a day
of ordinary proportions: blue sheets stripped
from the boy's bed to wash,
the long salmon pillow unzipped.
On the river, ice grown thin, and pale sun
through white mist that burns gold before it's done.
Woke, the boy, wound in joy:
a burrito on the floor, where laughing, he lay.

35 |

Of what is made   merriment? Or, Innate
first response, joy we learn to smother?
"Max could be a little less
enthusiastic." So. Another:
"Hopping to his cubby – not appropriate."
Fridays' small notes; we have to sign we see it.
Each day, we teach: laugh less
though *children* we must *like,* to *be-come,* for heaven's sake.

36 |

Under the green almonds, on the black sands,
from the crumbling cliff, you dug chunks of white stone
marbled and veined of pale green.
Gems and *emeralds* weighted
your pockets down, walking back the damp channel.
Mango, wild tamarind, air thick as flannel
where mosquitoes moan.
Magnetic, the sands volcanic inside your hands.

37 |

Until we make late February. Snow's
shake-down cancels plans: Thursday, now Friday.
Strains, through the walls,
your father's banjo as you build
your mine-craft house of red-stone, pen your smiling pink square pig
under rectangle clouds. For what do you dig,
deep in the gig-a-byte halls
of an imagined under-earth? For what secret, scentless rose?

38 |

Heavy in the boughs, still, the pristine snow.
A kind of yearning has hold of me – to dance,
said Sappho's old notebook:
and to look upon the lotus banks
of Acheron. Odd myth's deep river – memory.
But above our own river —Real, unfolding story –
calling, the male chickadees ease spring
with increasing frequency, *hey sweetie:* high, their notes, then low.

39 |

In the Living Room, the staple gun claps
metal mesh to wood on the tall structure:
a five-foot rat mansion
replete with three levels, and ramps to lure
the beloved pet for whom he did us adjure,
with tears and argument, his right to care
for a creature, his own, 'til we could not bear
to hold, from him, his set heart
and, shredding old lessons, began to make bedding from scraps.

40 |

Crystals sprung from cold air, shimmer, in sun,
as mist rises between ice islands.
Time-out in the half-bath.
Stay there all day! My husband yells.
His fingers drum – my son's – on the hollow door
as I dip a dirty glass in suds, pour.
I bend my head. *Please, mend.*
Burns hard, my heart, I would—not run.

41 |

I sing what you cannot hear in spoken words:
because I would for you give life sweet ease
help, Lord, me, to know, *how.*
More than—anything—I love, because, my boy,
you of heart – mine – and bones – made & honed, joy.
I'm hungry, you call. *Please.*
On the yellow rooster plate, the eggs scrambled into curds.

42 |

Searching through work you've missed – snow, then sickness –
I find the sentences for Friday's tests:
the vocabulary
holds only these words: attempt, and fail.
Also, their variations in verb and noun.
Language creates the pathways, the brain's pulsing town.
In another language,
to–be–a–boy is a verb of bright & blinding quickness.

43 |

A verb-poem. In winter, he writes: Blossoms
of glory bloom/Sum[m]er is here at last I can/ Run
and play. I Max will play/
In the bright blue sky over/
The universe to the galaxy.
— Behind the road of milk, an unknown gravity
the Great Attractor —
pulls us, its mass more than the galaxies' parts or sums.

44 |

Of Morning: the gray rain on leaky eaves
easing, gives way to the ring of spring peepers.
The boy in my lap leaves
when I search a pencil from my purse.
But first, he tells me they curse four times
in *Shrek* the movie: *and I watched that* – crap
and damn – *and something worse* –
when I was four or five. Oh, Child, Believe.

45 |

September 21, 2012: you (five) over me rolled,
jabbing elbows into ribs,
and knee – to the stomach –
as waking, you, laughing, roll & roll: "now
all your troubles are gone" though I, to dream, cling
yet to a torso in which I melt, a shoulder-wing,
of rib & heart, the ache,
of honey: *come into me*, a voice I try to hold.

46 |

But by mid-day, you (at eight) have harnessed
your rats in colored yarn – red & yellow & green,
and walk them – one-by-one
on the lawn. They, cage-born, sniff & lean
against the moss on the rain-dark, furrowed bark
of honey locust. I think of Sartre
as I pull the first young weeds
from my front garden: free, what-you-are untarnished

47 |

by what-you-*would*-become. Un-willed
into your own essence, not yet
for every human
action, responsible. I – my hands
in the loose dirt (soft, damp) – am all-human,
making way, for flowers, the space to bloom in:
ages, eons, this Womb
from whom the fruits, we gather, from whom, we are filled.

48 |

Some actions *like water into sand vanish:*
but others? Mind, too, is made out of earth
and, to my mind, returns. . .
("I love it" my son says – I've mouthed aloud
some actions like water – as, composing, I,
over the words, bowed.) Outside, my husband sighs
from the high roof
before the screaks of the crowbar vanish.

49 |

"With all my heart," nuzzling his bedhead
against my arm as he, beside me, sits,
playing – past time – a game
of monkeys & balloons – 150 hits
to your base, and then, you're dead, he tells me,
 as red balloons stream around the yin-yang's sea.
"Not *dead;* instead, say out.
It's creepy, with the balloons —you know, like blood, red."

50 |

I feel like we're going to write poems all day.
The pencil gripped, he, for me, writes, this:
bal[l]oons of greatness/
float   they make/ more. I will stand/
in a super Bal[l]oon/ well [while] in fire [.]
"A rhyme?" He answers: I flew with fire/ from higher./
By the back porch, the band
of crocuses open gold in the good sun's ray.

51 |

Spring blinks. Then, August's amber light. The cicada
caught, on the sidewalk, in your green net.
Small winged, with tarnished gold
over black carapace & face;
three tiny ruby jewels — ocelli,
those simple eyes separating dark from light —
between the large compounds,
drops of black water reflecting our moving mosaic.

52 |

You do not remember the two in Nebraska
who hung, upside-down, from their split nymphs,
wing-buds wet, uncrumpling, bright white-green,
as, tender, the bodies vibrated.
After your nap we returned to the maple's trunk;
pulled upright, forelegs clung yet to their husks,
spread wings in each soft vein pulsed,
spread wings our breath touched, when —abracadabra!

53 |

and the bright blue blurred, in air, away. Ancient chant -
I create as I speak —that you (eight) waived
over your black hat, snap,
and, slipped, quick, the rat from the bag
hidden beneath the table into the hat,
tipped, then upright. "Da-daaa." But – *"Did you see that?"* –
you asked, after. And yes,
I say, I saw in the moment meant to enchant.

54 |

En-Chant, from Latin *incantare*. In: In,
on into toward. Within Bring
into, the Condition Of.
Canere – to sing, o canary – oh! present
in– Finitive! Or, recap: o enChant! O Bring!
into, oh, the within within, oh the condition *o singing!* –
sing the Ah! infinite, O Awe present.
My djinn whistler, bring me back   from the future's dim din.

55 |

The blue ball lies on the thick lawn, half-shadow,
half-sun. *Only love and love's ecstasy*
writes H.D., and we – changed
by the earth's wheel around the sun –
start early on the birthday cake: nine tiers for you, at nine.
Batter splatters as you lift the beaters to make lines,
parallel waves, spider's lacy
tracings; and though told no, you lick the yellow bowl.

56 |

The final tier, topped with a yin yang – is your design;
you tell me "the dots mean that in every light,
a little darkness
and in every darkness,
a little light." The edges bleed black sugar
into white buttercream. The cake leans. Hunger
leans; for this moment, less,
though later, the golden dog will die and we both will cry.

57 |

If I could, again: us, on the back deck, in sun,
early October & yellow walnut leaves
lift, sift down; our muscles
warm from sawing saplings, we sit and sip
your cranberry mix; through glass, watch pink shadows
on bared arms, cheek, on knees and dirt-smudged clothes
as the river, below, breaks into many suns, the sun.

58 |

Chimes in heavy wind. November's election.
We wound at the billionaire's win.
In morning's lap, your Fear:
"What if he bombs other countries
and they bomb us back?" My job to transform, now,
this narrative, allow compassion's vow
to see no evil king pin
but say, a man caring, bad, for attention.

59 |

I waited for you to say you love me,
my ninety-four-year-old grandfather
sings again. His breath catches
and wavers as his hand hovers
over his heart, "Twenty-five percent, gone –".
I too touch his heart. He's seeded his lawn,
hopes it comes up, come spring,
but says, "I never was good, musically."

60 |

His deafness first from the roar of airplanes,
teaching gunners for World War II,
is now nearly complete.
He reads our lips, makes guesses.
"But you—" my son's high violin cuts through –
then my blind grandmother beelines—"it's not true,
Don, – you are – musical."
So, he sings: *when I was twenty-one* (though voice wanes)

I had a lot of fun, but now I'm old and gray
and the fun has gone away. Rough-eyed,
red-voiced, he recovers:
. . . and I don't care. Jimmy crack corn,
Master's gone away. He laughs weakly. My son laughs.
Many voices rise and fall as warmth wafts
from the wall-heater
beside his leather recliner. He lays down his hearing aid.

Late March; I near forty years. New tulips
push red spears above the dogs' muddy graves.
I call the white pup away.
Winter illness has made us grave:
five days without power, then strep, the flu,
and ongoing, the idiocy: Trump's coup.
I would— engrave
upon the earth's shifting currents more than his quips

63 |

(would, of him, make a single blip) and trace
(instead) the returning line of tundra swans,
under shoulders, shadows,
and in their black beaks, the flight-calls
cacophonous trills, high and squeaky bike horns
that the bright & bitter air adorns.
Beneath, I look about the lawns
for shoots, then cut the quince, big-budded, for a vase.

64 |

To orient to earth. Live like a monk.
Columbine uncircles purple leaves near
the first celery frills
of bleeding heart.
What grows, grows first in the dark. In warm gunk
rich with de-cay. In microbes' magic trunk,
the silent, miniscule seeds sing
luxuriant form into being, made from dung.

65 |

Children, perhaps, more than any, know, their bones
too, are so formed, singing, for years, *poop poop!*
at any opening;
provocation; or not; it's *poop!*
until our eyes roll— do they know other words? –
as they scour the ground for deer scat, dog turds,
giggle as goats' tails lift *poop*
glistening dingleberries! oh such rapturous tones!

66 |

Black banana, bum-browny, butt-nut, corndogs.
Hiedegger says the poet's vocation
is to speak the earth. Give name
as Rilke named the things of the earth. Dirt.
Droppings. So they may be resurrected anew,
within us. *Praise this world*, ephemeral, dew
that dissolves into damp earth.
Dookie, fudge nugget, junglebug, mud bunny, load, loaf, log.

67 |

The butterflies are hatching in Dow Gardens'
greenhouse: painted ladies, ruby tipped page,
black and white paper kites.
Chrysalides swing in the clear stage,
chartreuse– orchid– buds; husks to transparence, dried.
My son, from a sugared red sponge, has pried
a blue morpho. It clings
closed-winged, to his shirt, granting— as if wonder pardons.

68 |

Another beats against the glass ceiling,
pressing its blue to the cold blue beyond.
Fluttering down, flashes
eyes then sky then eyes, as if – wand –
(ancient act) Vanishing among shafts, arboreal light
on the root-filled trail to the water's white
fall, where I, alone, stood at dawn:
reappearing, within, that old self, Kneeling.

69 |

A day of hardness in the heart, though I run
the wetland's thawed trail, wet-eyed in wan light.
The geese beat their wings,
scream as I pass each nesting site.
In my head, my son's song, made-up for me
three nights before: *sweetie-pie, sweeten for me;*
his low voice rasped & clung
like I sing, for him, Holiday's *willow weep*, some nights.

70 |

We walk the fort walls in Florida sun,
pose by old cannons cast with floral designs,
rub palms over coquina
quarried from Anastasia Island
centuries ago. Those first soldiers carved
ships into soft lime above their beds, starved
for home. In another room, more signs
of such sickness: Plains' prisoners scratched their Dance of Sun.

71 |

After dragging to Flagler's frog fountain,
after the Alligator Farm's missed zipline,
after the Castillo
and the beach— boogey-boarding,
after Mac'n Cheese; too late, we return
to St. George Street where the chandeliers burn
behind Magic's closed door.
In darkness, wipes, from his turned cheek, sadness's sharp mountain.

72 |

Home again, I walk the rounds, see what's grown
in our absence. Narcissus's yellow cups,
thickened, tulips' buds,
celadon tamarack tips
like a magician's softest paintbrushes.
Oh coy & gentle, that presence, hushes
all that's turned corrupt
with want; you, earliest & first, life, call us your own, call, us, home.

73 |

Some redbud saplings have not, I think, made it.
I inspect each limb for the telltale
black knobs at each notch;
some already have pushed out, paled
to purpura, though close still, like a crown arrayed;
they'll pop, on delicate stems, in days.
I'm afraid I've botched
a hacked limb on the big tree: see none thickened.

74 |

But no. Later, I make them out on high branches.
So, sometimes, my worries, fruitless, for you,
and all I have done amiss,
just as my own father rues
how he broke my will, turned me, he thinks, meek.
But I see you skimming the waves' thinnest wash – sleek
on your green board
unfazed—taught—by early falls.   For hours, he launches —

75 |

as his father sifts for shark's teeth among shells.
I reapply sunscreen, look lazily
through piles laid before me,
find rose petal tellins
worn translucent, and delicate arks,
lettered olive. Best, I like ones washed of marks;
milk moon snail, I keep,
its broken edges worn smooth in the endless swells.

76 |

The wind within the wind. I wake with this line,
last of the dream's poem, as light through white curtains
filters. Beside me – you –
wrapped in red fleece, asleep, still mine
as yellow minutes in the old clock
turn: 6:45. Your worn tiger, Paws, knocked
to the floor. I knew—
too big, now, but you held him last night for a time.

77 |

I go far away, to write. To Belgium.
You will not miss me, or think of me, much.
Savage!
you'll laugh, running with cousins, wild
through sun-lit rooms, over small-rocked island beaches,
carving your name in the wood where no one leashes.
In dusk, you'll paddle
out on still waves, while I, far, listen: hidden drum.

78 |

I would be – soft-est breath upon your need.
Laying in the tide stones, gulping hard air,
some cousin's slight:
"I just want—to be—normal!"
as waves crest & break. I mean how, crowning, the light
comes through – by water's refractions made – more bright
before it falls to foam.
I pick through words, hope for something on which you can feed.

79 |

At nine, you come, most, to me, hurt or angry.

You've lost something, or something's broken: my fault;

I don't come quick enough

when you stub your toe, spill the salt,

catch the tadpole. It's not an easy role;

soother, watcher, blame-taker: takes a toll –

to en-Compass,

un-disturb-able as cloud, when wind shakes the Tree.

80 |

Dresses vest & tie; stage-lit – first – magic act.

Not magnificent, *Just Max* & his silver

bag a man's card goes in.

Brusque wave; the man pulls out pieces

of rope. *That's not what I asked for*! Classic gag.

Then, from air: long—unfurled—uncut, the bag

turned inside out,

only the black lining, empty, the contents jacked.

81 |

The Narrow roads I walk, outside Olsene,
(cut rye, gathered, drying in striped piles)
until I reach fence & deer.
Sika, white spotted. I stand very still
and think how, for days: the panther, Rilke
watching. Velvet-antlered, the buck comes close,
raises high his neck, the skin above his nose
wrinkling, as it does
when he mouths the short dry grass for what he can glean.

82 |

My son, as I so—love the quiet immeasurable eyes
of the young buck, I want to believe
we can cross over, cross between
some greeting   *I see you   I see*
you here at four: watch me watch me always
as you swing, spinning summer   in a blue haze.
The Watcher—to Believe—
watches no transcendence beyond, no heavenly guise

83 |

when by me in the dusk my child sits down
and I, smaller, am yet allowed and fold him in my arm.
I Ache, that made body
and body's Border   that now from me
quickly quickly   Goes. Old story. Cliché
cast of mold, cast of hardened lime and clay,
that many may read
our deepened print, pressed hard, around this thorn & crown.

84 |

Play with me Play with me Play with me *as if* A
is B. Be Kallepae be Daddy
Zebra   be Silly
spilling his little cup of tea.
No me comprendes squeaks green Lizardo
who loves to make metaphors but not to sew
while Hopster gutter-
glots "Welcome to the Pit of Despair," and headbangs.

85 |

By your works shall ye be known, my paper-folder,
in   dove light   paper light   my tea ceremony
my gorgeous sentence
undone. You, overtakelessness,
who of me makes a chiming, a nothing
roving in gentían light, bent & unbent,
as branches Touch the wind, of cranes swiftly sent
who yet are far from nest, & rest —
I mean to say, touch this thing I've made from paper.

86 |

The little pieces that once belonged
to a whole: snaps unsewn to fabric,
a child's scissors,
scrap of map, or a small key
to no known door. The photograph's film worn
and scraped till the child's face is erased.
May I, with these, adorn
the stalk, which dry, and shaken, from kernels yet come song.

87 |

A kind of intoxication, rising up
as if through water: blues, translucent,
shift & shimmer—like sequins shimmer—
with light toward, pierced with, from
the greater   light. Close to, rising up, a kind
of surface, nameless, or named, with light, lined,
a kind of shimmer,
up the body goes   those who drown, a kind of   up.

88 |

But you, my child —no boats, crowded, un-vested,
no cold borders, or border guards; yet, each
child given, could be, my keeping.
Each encircling, anxious arm,
my arm. Once "Mother" —though I enact my own
Lassitudes— I am, of Multitudes: no zone
of Exclusion. Give
how, kicking, the sparks' dimming shines; then, is rested.

89 |

I hang, on the line, laundry's smell like wind,
lavender-tinged & willow, white-scented, silvering
undersides to rain's
coming. My fingers, clipping cloth
to wooden pins, seem over-knuckled, big; bloom
with colors unnamed, & veined. Not as noum–
ena, *a thing in itself,*
but of senses, wholly, as the wind grows big, kin.

90 |

I would for you make the kind world.
A map of the compassionate Day:
to go where you love
and where you are loved, as I, to grasses, go.
Here we are, in June water; *on three? —So, on*
five. Together, our heads go under. Gone,
the Self, shocked, by now knows
the pure right bright wash so cold loosens it all our quarrels.

91 |

Near evening. Long-limbed, tawny, lacquered shadows
lay in the fragrance of damp grass and flax.
We are moving the ladder.
I unhinge, and lock the red slats
steady. Our quail, penned, call quiet *reet reet.*
To lilac, pales the earth, exhales the heat.
The small candle inside
the jar, high on the branch. The next, yet in shadow.

92 |

I dream sadness: the farm—accumulation;
my mother's mother's clothes in boxes
nineteen years after death.
If I hold to them, they are still here
my mother says. Chipped jar, inkwell carried
under the shirt, warmed, with oranges, ferried
miles through Christmas snow. Dear,
the daughter, five lifetimes ago. Let go. Not your ration.

46

93 |

Fever-gaunt, trembling, short of breath to speak,
Edith Schiele scrawled, on scrap paper,
her last: ". . . love . . . more and more
infinite. . . immeasurable,"
her husband sketching: black crayon, quick, poor,
his last: her eyes gilded, glazed with (. . .*no more*)
the babe inside her.
Her right hand, ringed, fingers splayed loose against the cheek.

94 |

A child: two things frighted me. First— (second?)
reincarnation. The hill scooped for gravel,
my sister's rose face,
the black of mailbox unraveled,
racked, as I, *I could not* compass such—*sob*—cruelty
dissolved all loves, where lay one's fealty.
Never—know her face.
The other— earlier, I think now, sudden, stunned

me half-way down the gravel, rain-rutted, drive,
running, released from the cruel school bus
when thought, I, of, straight-down,
China, dug & out – where? There was
a girl I did not know. Then, hard, sharp tug
while I, riveted, could not move. The rug,
as if, wracked from under,
I realized, *separate,* severed, became so, with that knife.

The not-me. I walked then, strange in this stark
body. A great emptiness where had been,
moments before, others
like me, who I wóuld know. Kin, ken.
I picked my way carefully down the drive
where each small stone gleamed, seemed distinct, a-live;
felt— my body's borders,
a heavy lightness; my shadow clear; the bright, dark, dread.

97 |

Learning to speak, you would mirror our words,
and so, of yourself, spoke second-person:
"*You* [meaning I] want more."
And I, for years, of myself, made third:
"Momma. . . will do the dishes. Momma's done."
There was no *I* between us, only one and one
over and overing
god's eye silvering gods-us us between our silver herds

98 |

as silver drops from sunlight through shutter
lucent blue & wheat green, poppy woven,
we slept, half-slept, hammocked
& hushed, outside, mostly, of language,
in the sweet space of milk and milk's leafed lips
where love over-roved, proved, my peach, my pips,
my little chicken
peeps. O butter, brain, I—udders, unsundered Utter.

Big elephant hang up towel, you said
pointing to the picture. Full, first, sentence.
Of Always, unbound
by Time & time's delineations—
oh what have we Taught. My heart walks, will walk – away, in world,
and I, my open chest, stand it— unfurled, purled
by ravages of air.
Always: rocket, moon, slender star *want milk go home* be, fed.

ACKNOWLEDGMENTS

Deep gratitude to the editors of the following journals where stanzas from this book previously appeared: *Conjunctions, Poetry Northwest, Birmingham Poetry Review, Antioch Review,* and *Poetry International.*

This work was supported, during a critical stage, through a Dickinson House Fellowship; thank you, Éireann Lorsung, for your gift of beautiful time, space, company. So grateful, also, to my Dickinson House cohort, Asiya Wadud and Su Hwang: your work and your presences.

This work was also sustained by the Ruth and Ted Braun Fellowship Program, endowed by the Harvey Randall Wicks Foundation. Profound gratitude for this sponsorship.

Vast thanks to the whole Milkweed team: to Daniel Slager for believing in the poem, to Mary Austin Speaker for her enthusiasm and artistic vision, for the many caring editorial hands: Lee Oglesby, Kathryn Nuernberger, Bailey Hutchinson, Tijqua Daiker. For all the others who helped bring this into being, and into the world, including Joanna D. Demkiewicz, Claire Laine, Shannon Blackmer, and Milan Wilson-Robinson.

In loving memory of my grandfather Donald Ross (1922 – 2019) who departed during this book's time. In loving appreciation for those still here.

Thank you, most, always, to my son Max, my patient co-conspirator, who gave me permission.

And, for my husband: this is possible because of you.

Anna Swartz

ARRA LYNN ROSS is the author of *Seedlip and Sweet Apple*. She is a poet, essayist, and occasional puppet worker whose work has appeared in *Conjunctions, Passages North, Fourth Genre, River Teeth, Denver Quarterly, Poetry Northwest, Prairie Schooner, Birmingham Poetry Review, Antioch Review,* the *Iowa Review, Bennington Review,* and other places. She lives on the Pine River in Michigan.

milkweed
editions

Founded as a nonprofit organization in 1980, Milkweed Editions is an independent publisher. Our mission is to identify, nurture and publish transformative literature, and build an engaged community around it.

Milkweed Editions is based in Bdé Óta Othúŋwe (Minneapolis) within Mní Sota Makhóčhe, the traditional homeland of the Dakhóta people. Residing here since time immemorial, Dakhóta people still call Mní Sota Makhóčhe home, with four federally recognized Dakhóta nations and many more Dakhóta people residing in what is now the state of Minnesota. Due to continued legacies of colonization, genocide, and forced removal, generations of Dakhóta people remain disenfranchised from their traditional homeland. Presently, Mní Sota Makhóčhe has become a refuge and home for many Indigenous nations and peoples, including seven federally recognized Ojibwe nations. We humbly encourage our readers to reflect upon the historical legacies held in the lands they occupy.

milkweed.org

Interior design by Tijqua Daiker and Mary Austin Speaker
Typeset in Bembo

Bembo was created in the 1920s under the direction
of printing historian Stanley Morison for the Monotype
Corporation. Bembo is based upon the 1495 design cut by
Francesco Griffo for Aldus Manutius, and named after the first book to
use the typeface, a small book called *De Aetna*,
by the Italian poet and cleric Pietro Bembo.